Lucky
Numbers

Iris Howden

Published in association with
The Basic Skills Agency

Hodder & Stoughton
A MEMBER OF THE HODDER HEADLINE GROUP

Orders: please contact Bookpoint Ltd, 39 Milton Park, Abingdon, Oxon
OX14 4TD. Telephone: (44) 01235 400414, Fax: (44) 01235 400454.
Lines are open from 9.00-6.00, Monday to Saturday, with a 24 hour message
answering service. Email address: orders@bookpoint.co.uk

British Library Cataloguing in Publication Data
Howden, Iris
   Lucky numbers. – (Chillers) (Livewire)
   1. Readers – English fiction
   I. Title   II. Basic Skills Agency
   428.6

ISBN 0 340 697598

First published 1997
Impression number   10 9 8 7 6 5 4 3
Year   2005 2004 2003 2002 2001 2000 1999

Typeset by Fakenham Photosetting Ltd, Fakenham, Norfolk.
Printed in Great Britain for Hodder & Stoughton Educational,
a division of Hodder Headline Plc, 338 Euston Road, London NW1 3BH
by Athenæum Press Ltd, Gateshead, Tyne & Wear.

Lucky Numbers

Contents

1	Lottery Dreams	1
2	Roll-over	5
3	Picking Numbers	8
4	Jackpot!	11
5	No Answer	18
6	Bad News	22

1

Lottery Dreams

I did the lottery at work.

I did it with the lads.

They were Lee, Jacko and Sid.

We did it every Friday.

We each gave Sid a pound.

On Saturday he went shopping.

He bought the lottery tickets then.

We knew we could trust Sid.

He was a good bloke,

older than the rest of us.

You could rely on Sid.

He helped me when I started work.

He looked after me.

We all chose the numbers.

We kept the same ones each week.

I chose two dates –

my birthday and my wedding day.

Jacko chose his car number

and his age.

Sid chose his car number

and his age as well.

Lee had numbers on pieces of paper.

He just stuck a pin in.

We talked about winning.

We talked about spending the money.

'I'd have a good holiday', Lee said.

Maybe go to Hong Kong.'

'I'd buy a big, flash car,' Jacko said.

'Drive the girlfriend to London.

Go to all the top clubs.

What about you, Kev?'

'I'd buy my own house', I said.

'New clothes for us,

toys for the kids.

Pay off the bills.'

'I'd put it in the bank,' Sid said.

'Invest it. Live off the interest.'

2

Roll-Over

But we never had a big win.

Now and again we won a tenner.

Sid would pick up the money.

Then he shared it out with us.

'One day, lads,' he would say.

'We'll win the big one. The jackpot.

Just you wait and see.'

One week there was a roll-over.

Nobody had won it before.

The jackpot stood at 40 million pounds.

People went mad buying tickets.

The shops were packed.

'Let's have an extra go.

It's worth it this week,' Sid said.

'Let's put in an extra 25p.

We'd get an extra ticket.

A one-off.'

So we did that.

3

Picking
Numbers

'How shall we do the extra ticket?'

'It doesn't matter', Sid said.

'We'll all choose.

Pick your lucky numbers.'

'I'll have 8 and 28.' Ted said.

'And I'll have 7 and 13.' Jacko said.

'What's your lucky number, Kev?'
Sid asked. I thought for a bit.
Then I said '39'.
'OK', Sid said.
He got a slip of paper.
He wrote down 7, 8, 13, 28 and 39.

'We need one more number,' Sid said.
'It should be higher. What about 44?'
We all agreed. Sid wrote it down.

Sid took our money.
He took out an envelope.
He put in a five pound note.
And the slip of paper.
We wrote our names on the front.
'I'll get the tickets on Saturday.'

4

Jackpot!

On Saturday night I was at home.

I liked to watch the draw on TV.

Meeta was upstairs.

She was putting the kids to bed.

Eight o'clock came. The show began.

I got the numbers out of my coat.

I put them in front of me.

A woman came on.

She was wearing a mini-dress.

A star guest came on to sing.

'Hurry up, Meeta,' I shouted.

'The draw is on soon.'

The star pushed the button.

The balls began to spin.

The first ball out was 28.

'Good old Lee,' I said.

I ticked the 28 in front of me.

The next one was 7.

'Yes!' I shouted. 'That's one more.'

I ticked the 7.

Next out was my number, 39.

Three numbers – we'd won a tenner.

Meeta came into the room.

'How are we doing?' she asked.

'Shhh!' I said.

The fourth ball was coming out.

It was the number 13.

'We've got four numbers!' I shouted.

'Keep your fingers crossed, Meeta.'

Number 8 rolled out.

I grabbed Meeta.

I hugged and kissed her.

'Five numbers. We could have won
thousands!'

Meeta was laughing and clapping.

We stood still to watch the last ball.

I crossed my fingers.

One more ball to go.

I held my breath. I waited.

It was number 44. Sid's number.

I could not believe my eyes.

'Let's check again,' I said.

Meeta read out the numbers from
my slip of paper.

I pointed to each one on the TV.

'We've done it!' I shouted.

'We've won the jackpot!'

Meeta was jumping with joy.

I hugged her.

We danced round the room.

I was singing at the top of my voice –

'We're in the money!'

The phone rang. It was Lee.

'Am I right?' he said.

'Have we won? Am I dreaming?'

'You're right,' I said.

'We've won the jackpot!

I can hardly believe it.'

'Shall we ring the others?' he asked.

'Yes, you ring Jacko.

I'll ring Sid,' I said.

'I'll see you on Monday.

I'm still going to work.

Sid has to ring up the lottery firm.

I want to be there then.'

5

No Answer

I rang Sid many times that evening.

There was no reply.

I tried again the next morning.

There was still no answer.

'He'll be out having a good time,' said Meeta.

'Let's take the kids out and have fun.'

So we did just that.

We took the kids out for Sunday lunch.

Then we went to the fun fair.

We had a great time.

As soon as I got back I tried Sid again.

Still no answer.

It seemed very odd.

I spoke to the others.

'I hope he hasn't done a bunk,' said Lee.

'Maybe he wants to keep the money.'

'Not Sid,' I said. 'We can trust him.

He wouldn't run off.'

'I can't understand it,' said Jacko.

'Why hasn't he rung?

Where can he be?'

I didn't know what to say.

By now I was worried.

It wasn't like Sid.

'We'll find out at work on Monday,' I said.

I didn't sleep well.

I kept tossing and turning.

Meeta was very quiet.

She knew something was wrong.

6

Bad News

Sid did not turn up for work.

It began to look bad.

No-one knew where he was.

Then someone came in to see the boss.

It was Darren. He was Sid's son.

The boss led him over to us.

'Darren's got some very bad news,' he said.

'I'm afraid Sid is dead.'

We were all stunned.

'What happened?' I asked.

'My dad was run over,' Darren said.

It happened on Saturday in town.

He was hit by a number 44 bus.

He died in hospital. Mum was with him.

She found this in his pocket.

It has your names on it.'

He handed the envelope to me.

Darren left. I opened the envelope.

Inside was the fiver and the slip of paper.

Our lucky numbers were on it –

7, 8, 13, 28, 39 and number 44.

'Poor Sid, he was such a good man.
He must have been on his way
to buy the ticket,' I said.

We were all quiet.
I tore up the slip of paper.
The number 44 fell on the floor
in front of me.
I picked it up and held it tight.
I had to stop myself from crying.
The money didn't matter –
Sid had been like a father to me.
I missed him already.

'They're unlucky numbers now,' said Lee.